Good to
GREAT
GRANT WRITING

Secrets to Success

JULIE CWIKLA PHD

"Be so good they can't ignore you."

Steve Martin

PROLOGUE

I've written this quick read for people like me, a younger me driving hard on the tenure track or sweating on the proposal treadmill. You need insight from someone who's been there, someone who will be straight with you, someone you can trust. By the way, I'm still in the grant writing game, and it's always a challenge. But I think therein lies the fun in all of this.

Every RFP (request for proposals) is a chance for me to sell my new idea. And new ideas are continually forming with emerging research, new partnerships, and fresh colleagues. It's an everchanging landscape and a challenge to navigate.

I'm stopping my game for a hot minute, to share and collect solid reminders, strategies, hints, and ways I've worked to set my proposals apart – and take the lead in the stack of wannabe funded projects.

Grant writing is a game.

And we grant developers and the funding agencies are on the same team (remember that). We are all trying to do good, to advance knowledge, and to support our communities.

Nevertheless, there are winners, losers, scores, rules and an audience. The competition is fun and the winning sweet. The money buys you materials, assistance, space, travel, and sometimes most importantly, time.

Time, time, time.

We all want more time – time to read, to think, and to write. Writing, "good writing" is one of the most important of all human products. And a winning proposal has the potential to support larger more ongoing products that influence future proposals, products ... It's an onion. But it's demanding work to put together a great project in your mind and then squeeze your ambitious 5-year plan into less than 20 single spaced pages.

An undergrad math professor called mathematics the "lazy man's language." Mathematicians are so succinct and efficient that tremendous notions that require pages of English to describe can be communicated with a few symbols - *condensing great ideas into the tiniest of space.*

This is precisely the game of grant writing. Cramming your huge idea, perhaps decades of background literature, and years of future work into a short document.

You're busy. You know the basics already. You feel like you should be writing right now. But you want to take your grant game to the next level.

This is a book of notes and essential reminders I tell myself organized into three parts:

Art
Architecture
Attitude

I hope they help you too.

ACRONYMS

When you dip your foot into the grant writing world, it's kind of like entering the military. Acronyms – They are EVERYWHERE. So I'm listing the few I'll use in this book just in case.

RFP = Request for Proposals – This is the document agencies release when they have money to award. It has all the specifics, rules, budget limits, due dates, guidelines, page length, etc.

PI = Principal Investigator – This is the project's lead researcher.

SPO = Sponsored Program Office – Your organization's staff or office that helps PIs submit grant proposals and manage funds post award. If you are a small non-profit or school district you might not have this support.

Part One

ART

The application of human creative skill and imagination.

TELL THE PUNCHLINE FIRST

What's your hook? Your elevator speech? Think of grant writing like screenwriting or journalism. Grab the reader by the heart, look them in the eyes, and make them feel the importance of your work. Who is this going to save, who is going to care, why will this be important 20 years from this moment? Is your heart racing? This is the grant game!

In most academic writing – reports, journal articles, monographs – researchers introduce the work, place it in the field appropriately, perhaps provide historical context, slip in some accolades, maybe some Ivy pedigree, this or that.

With a grant – get to it – this is business.

Tell the punchline first.

I don't know the punchline until I've written the whole proposal. Then I use 1-3 sentences right at the opening – that's your punchline. You've digested, regurgitated, and edited the hell out of the 20 pages over the past six months. Now you're ready to collapse, synthesize and spit it out in one breath.

Make it good. Grab the reader on your first shot. Grab them!

An ideal punchline will:

1. Evoke emotion.

2. Create credibility.

3. Inspire action.

Punchlines or introductory sentences are the hardest things to write – You've just walked on stage. Everybody's looking at you. Your work is complex and detailed. Summarizing it into three sentences - a ridiculous task!

This part is always – always – hard.

But you are never wasting time thinking about these opening lines because they are never really finished. Write these last when you are breathing, sleeping, dreaming your project. But - Be thinking about them *always*.

WRITE TO SELL

Writing a research proposal or grant request is different from any other type of writing. Most academic writing is a report, a reflection of what you've already done, learned, accomplished. There might be some allusion to future work or a call to action. But it's a report, the work is in the past.

In a grant proposal you're not reporting, you're selling.

You're selling your research idea, your future plan, your team's potential. And the reviewers are your buyers. Some of these reviewers are in your field, others tangential, others even further afield. But this is a thoughtful audience and they are looking for a pet project, good work to champion and push forward. They are knowledgeable, broad minded, noted in their field, and giving their time to serve an agency as a reviewer. This is a learned group of individuals with their own biases and leanings they bring to the table.

Your job: Reach them all.

Impress them all.

Sell your idea so well they simply can't say no.

GRANT WRITING IS MARKETING

You're thinking about what you want – of course, you are – money to cover your summers, a new piece of equipment so you can extend your research program, assistance in the lab from students and post docs, a line on your vitae, a step closer to tenure perhaps.

Now, stop thinking about you!

Think about the agency.

How you can help THEM get what they want?

You must hold their mission and your goals in your mind at the same time.

Craft a project to meet the needs of both.

Unlike a dissertation - the goal here is to sell. You are selling your program idea and you want them to buy it. They simply won't buy a product they don't like or need.

Instead speak to their mission statement, specifics of the RFP. Understand and link to work they've previously funded.

This is not about you.

This is about cultivating a relationship via words and ideas. A relationship and research partnership that will achieve the agency's mission.

BE A STORYTELLER

If you're like me, you were trained as a scientist. You took the English classes because you had to, wrote precise gorgeous outlines you fleshed into well-structured paragraphs and got all As.

But have you ever written a story?

A real story?

Words that entertain?

Deductive reasoning, logic, if-then statements are all effective frameworks for your research design and methods. But to tell a compelling story - a story a reviewer wants to champion – you need an arc, a conflict, a hero, and a dash of drama. Capture the need for the work and touch their heart with the broader impact of the work.

Why is your science worthy of exploration?

What is some crazy way off place it might touch and change?

Who will be affected by your work both short term and long term?

Your work is important. And you are an excellent researcher that can change the field and influence others on your path.

Tell that great story of the future.

VISION

Stop your tunnel vision.

Too often those seeking funding are so deep in their work, crunched for time, and accustomed to writing for a highly specialized academic audience they forget to look up. With a degree in field A, subgroup B, specializing in C, they don't shift gears and think of the larger audience involved in reviewing and funding proposals.

No matter the agency – National Science Foundation, EPA, state Department of Education, private foundation – the readers and reviewers are real people. They are often scientists, specialists, or educators in your field but might be somewhat tangential to your work or work in other non-profit or profit arenas. Picture these people and their perspectives while you're writing.

The audience is not as narrow as a journal referee panel.

Look up.

Look wide.

Write.

PICTURE YOUR READER

Always picture your reader. You're not writing a memoir for your soul. You're describing a project to win over the reader. Write for your audience.

When someone reads a journal article you've written, they found the piece because it was in their field of interest, maybe it was cited in an article they were reading, and they subscribe to that journal because it's eminent in their area and they read it cover to cover each issue. In other words, they already like and are well versed on the subject. They want to understand and learn about your new findings. They know it will be good because it's published in the Magnificent Journal that has a 1.8% acceptance rate. This is what a happy interested reader looks like.

Now picture a reader reviewing your great new idea packaged in a grant proposal submitted to Research on Wheels (ROW). Their job is to critique and whittle down their stack, quantitatively and qualitatively assessing and perhaps ranking them in some manner that aligns with the goals and mission of ROW.

Your research design, goals, and purpose must be better than anyone else in that stack.

You must SELL your idea faster and better than anyone else submitting their great idea.

You are not writing to a journal editor or your dissertation advisor or your grandmother – that sassy thing who is fascinated with your latest patent and reads everything you write.

You are marketing your idea to all of the following:

- A fatigued reviewer sitting among a pile of proposals, who knows, he should be writing his own stuff right now.

- A Full Professor who is on vacation, looking to be inspired and excited by her list of new proposals written mostly by brilliant junior faculty members. She loves reviewing grant proposals.

- Crazy efficient researcher juggling a lab, kids, the tenure track, and 10 graduate students.

Keep their attention. Do not bore the readers.

Reviewers are just like you and me. Write to them and connect with them as soon as you can.

REVIEWERS ARE PEOPLE TOO

The reviewers have a life just like you. Maybe they are a single mom like I was, a new professor getting review panel experience, a full professor looking to support an edgy new concept, or a director of a large non-profit.

Your goal is to evoke emotion in the reader. Make them feel. Create a need. Communicate your passion for this work and the timeliness of the project – this one tiny brick you're painstakingly spending your life to add to the academic wall of knowledge.

Why is it so important?

You know why!

You're taking hours, days, and weeks to get money to do more of it. And it's probably what you've studied since you were 18. Convince the reader this needs to be done now, it aligns with the agency mission and you're the *best person* to lead the work.

WHO LOVES JARGON?

My adviser would say, "Write so your mother can understand it." My mother was an intelligent woman, so this was not a perfect mantra for me but nevertheless it sticks. My advisor's been uber successful because his writing is so clear, walking the reader from evidence to evidence so that you almost begin questioning, "Why didn't I write this?"

Every field has jargon. I won't bore you with any. The point is - Don't use it! You are selling an idea. Make it clear to the reviewer why they should invest in you and your work. Terminology is of course required, but jargon turns a reader off. Stop the madness.

PS. I don't mean acronyms, I mean "high faluting mumbo jumbo" – the flowery jargon. Think Hemingway. Every word matters. Don't waste any of your writing real estate on jargon.

HEMINGWAY

Speaking of Hemingway … When the New York Times reviewed *The Sun Also Rises* they wrote,

"It is a truly gripping story, told in lean, hard athletic prose."

Has a better review ever been written?

That's what you're shooting for in grant writing.

LEAN

HARD

ATHLETIC

You want your words, every single word working for you. You want to be succinct and efficient and use your available page count to tell as much of your story as possible. Choose strong words that do your heavy lifting and convince a reviewer of the project's worthiness.

EVERY WORD MATTERS

I can't stress this enough. Every word matters. Make every word count. When you are living and breathing your work it's easy to lose focus because it's second nature to you.

Get some distance. This might mean, put it down for a while, go for a walk, get some sleep, go on vacation.

Read your words as if an outsider to the work. Sit in a different chair. Read in a new location. Read it aloud. Stop on EACH word. Examine it. Does it clarify and contribute to the question you are investigating?

In your method section are the plans and work flow clear and sequential? When I'm reviewing my own document, I imagine I'm going to hand this to a colleague once it's funded – because I'm dead or better yet get called to Paris for five years. Is there enough detail for someone else to see the project through to completion?

Although every word matters, don't let this stunt your writing habit. When you are sketching, drafting and writing, every word you type is getting you closer to the final artifact.

> "Lower your standards and keep lowering them until the flow begins. Those nasty judges in our heads don't belong there until the very end when it's time to edit and rewrite."
> – Tina Welling

Don't constrain idea flow. Know there will be layers of shaping and editing. A final proposal is a refined artifact. It is months of writing your ideas in the most succinct format.

MORE FOREST ...

Because I am a lover of metaphor and symbolism – as a writer I think about the forest and the trees.

Your reviewers will not know all the species of trees in your forest, how or where they grow. When you begin, entice the reader with the beautiful forest, big wide panorama of your work, where it fits globally, and why more investigation is needed and worthy* of support.

Then walk them into the forest, describe the history of the forest, how you got here, the trees of interest. Every once and a while zoom out briefly again to the forest. But keep diving deep into the work and demonstrate your expertise.

This is a careful cadence of zooming in and zooming out to illuminate the trees but carefully maintain the forest's image, the "what's possible?" backdrop in the reader's mind.

* See that word "worthy" – it made you care, right? It invoked a whiff of morality and almost made you sit up straighter. Use powerful words to influence your reader.

... MORE TREES

All that business about More Forest ... Many proposals get rejected simply because they lack specificity and details.

Get nitty gritty and specific especially when justifying and grounding the research questions and detailing the methods. Details can often be crammed into tables for the more discerning reviewers and you can often times get away with a smaller font here as well. The devil is in the details and reviewers will want to know you've thought about how the results of Experiment A will impact B or how many interviews and focus groups you'll conduct with principals about the new curriculum.

Just remember, give the reader little respites by zooming out and reminding them of the research's broader impacts and how it's all rooted together.

QUESTIONS FOR THE READER

Want to entertain, educate, and entice your reader? You want them to be inspired and intrigued by your idea, right?

Give them questions along the way.

But how would the new enzyme perform in cold climates?

What options would keep our students persisting in physics?

Why is this critical to cardiac performance in deep-sea fish?

Questions make readers feel part of the work.

Remember the "Choose Your Own Adventure" series? Why were they so popular? They gave the reader choice, control, terrific immersion and involvement for young readers.

Questions break up dense descriptions, text, and analyses you no doubt must include. They also trigger pause and reflection. And they force *engagement with your project*.

A properly worded question can evoke emotion and ideally action – *Action* to label your work as a frontrunner.

What kind of questions will you ask?

CONVERSATION

Think of your proposal as a regulated conversation. Conversations often abide by unstated terms of agreement. At a cocktail party, I ask you about your life, you ask about mine, we often seek topics of shared interest and might delve deeper in discussion. Or we might bore each other after understood formalities are exchanged and leave to refresh our adult beverage.

With a grant proposal there is a writer, a reader, and an RFP to guide the conversation.

(1) You, the writer, actively agreed to enter the grant competition understanding the rules and regulations.

(2) The reader is a paid or unpaid reviewer for an agency who agreed to read ideas that adhere to those rules (topic, length, budget).

You agree to write, educate, inform, and hopefully entice your reader. The reader agrees to read and evaluate based on the rules. This agreement is an opportunity for you to get your idea in front of another scholar's eye balls.

It's an audition.

The more you can make your proposal a conversation with another scholar that educates, informs, and entices, the more likely you'll get funded.

Like any piece of writing it is a combination both of *what* you write and *how* you write it. Make your proposal a conversation the reader is happy they joined and forgets their drink is running low.

BREATH TEST

People laugh when I mention this in workshops but it's the straight truth.

If you must take a breath while reading a sentence it's simply too long.

I suggest reading all your writing out loud. Hearing your words in your ears is different than in your mind. It will help with timing, cadence, and those nasty run on sentences. It will also help you vary sentence length. Too many short sentences together sound choppy, too many long ones in a row tires the reader. Variety is the spice of life as they say.

In addition to structure it helps curb other issues like posturing and dryness often found in proposals. If you feel awkward or coy or corny saying a sentence out loud – it needs attention and revision.

PART TWO

ARCHITECTURE

The practice of designing and constructing

THE HOURGLASS

The shape and function of the hourglass helps organize proposals – the audience for each section, the flow, the cadence, and the structure.

An hourglass is widest at the top, narrow at the neck or middle, and similarly wide again at the bottom. This structure controls the sand's speed of flow. It also captures a before, during, and after. A visual of the passage of time and flow – and in our case information. It can also be inverted and reused indefinitely – a lovely symmetry.

Vertical pairs of triangles or cones connect at an apex. That apex is the *heart* of the proposal – the pinnacle – the ultimate summary of the work – the **Research Questions**.

The base of the triangles or the top and bottom of the hourglass bulbs are your introduction and conclusion. These sections need to speak to the broadest audience and make connections to a larger framework or context. These are the "Who cares?" Why is this work important for the funder, the field, region, country? This is your punchline! Tell it in the introduction and retell in the conclusion.

Each section that takes you to and from these "global conversations" at the beginning and the end, to the apex get progressively more specific and detailed.

SHAPE OF
GREAT GRANT WRITING

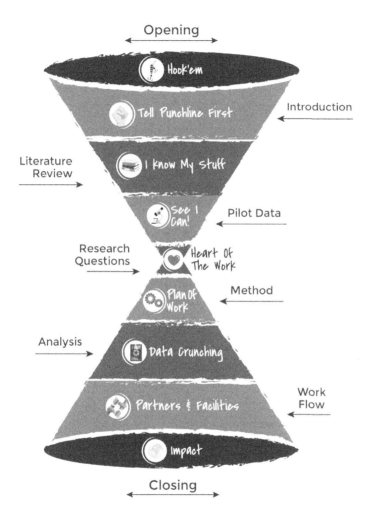

START WITH A BIG IDEA

People always ask me where to start.

Start with your idea.

What do you want to understand?

What you want to accomplish?

Who do you want to serve?

How will you measure progress?

Why do you care about this work?

I do not suggest starting with the RFP because then you end up trying to people please and not truly developing your project. After you have some ideas sketched then identify some sources for funding all or pieces of the work.

Work through the above questions in an idea notebook. And keep reworking them. Your interests and paths will change regularly. Never be afraid to start sketching a new idea because you feel committed or tied to a previous idea. Some ideas need to be discarded, maybe not completely, but the timing might not be right, or a new collaboration is driving you in a new direction. Don't be weighed down by past ideas. If you feel the drag of the ball and chain, the idea is no longer helping or exciting you – move on. Other idea resources and exercises are on my webpage as well.

RESEARCH QUESTIONS

The heart of the proposal is the research questions.

When reviewing a proposal, I typically read the summary or abstract and jump right to the research questions.

Every word matters.

Every word defined.

No jargon.

No ambiguity.

No extra words.

Everything flows from your research questions. These must be crystal – strong and clear.

What will we learn from this work?

The research questions are the proposal's essence, its core.

Any researcher should be able to grasp your proposal project from simply reading your research questions.

BACKGROUND AND LITERATURE REVIEW

Novice PIs tend to include too much background, thinking they need to begin with Stonehenge. This is not a dissertation. The reviewer simply needs some seminal pieces, the landmarks to communicate to a broader scope. Then dig and focus on the two to four dozen works that specifically have led to your new idea that takes the next step or fills a gap.

This section should illustrate the research steps that led to your new ideas and method to investigate. This is a great place to use questions to involve the reader. Such as, "Researchers were at a crossroads, how could we investigate birth weight and the repeated abnormalities?" The word "we" makes the reader feel part of the process, the work, part of your story that has led to your research questions.

Story – Your literature review and background tell the story of how you got here, why this is important, and demonstrate you are the absolute best person to make the next step.

Great novels, great movies, great biographies are all stories. I would argue the same for great proposals – Except the end is left unwritten until the money flows.

Wait, I need to be a thoughtful academic, a diligent scientist, and now a **story teller**? Yup!

- Think like a Professor
- Design like an Entrepreneur
- Write like Hemingway
- Craft like a Copyeditor

VISUAL SKETCHING

I often use sketching in my own grant development notebook to help me understand how work will flow, who will oversee these experiments, the data collection, storage, analyses. The sketching or mapping can also be useful for complicated theoretical relationships and describing how new theories will be tested and examined.

Concept maps and logic models can be a useful way to visually display your project's theories, complex relationships, or flow of work. Your thinking, the literature, and previous work that support your current idea can often be captured and better illustrated visually. Overlapping circles, flow chart tools and symbols can lead the reader through your process and methods. Some RFPs require a logic model that capture formative and summative evaluation components.

And regardless of requirements your reviewers will have different strengths and ways of interpreting information. Don't bore with redundancy but educate with multimodal presentations of your project theories and methods.

METHOD & ANALYSES

Begin with a calendar. This is a detailed part of your work where you help the reviewer understand what you're going to do each week or month. How will the work happen?

> What experiments will be conducted, in what order and why?

> What data are you collecting?

> Who will you hire and what will they do?

> When will you travel to present results or meet with a collaborator?

The details are tedious but necessary to illustrate you have thought through the HOW of your work. Show the reader you've got this covered.

This is a great section for tables, calendars, charts to summarize and illustrate work flow. Below are sketches that can help you move from research questions to objectives, to experiments, to budget. More examples and templates are available on my webpage.

RESEARCH QUESTIONS & HYPOTHESES

	Objective I	Objective II	Objective III
Month 1	Experiment A & B		
Month 2	Repeat trials A & B	Experiment C & D	Experiment C & E (depends outcome C)
Month 3		Experiment C2 & D2	
Month 4			Experiment E & F
Month 5			
Month 6			

Activities

RESEARCH QUESTIONS & HYPOTHESES

	Obj I	Methods	Obj II	Methods	Obj III	Methods
M1	Exp A & B	IRT2				
M2	Re A & B	IRT2/3	Exp C & D	A3Z	Exp C & E (dep C)	S-DENSE
M3			Ex C2 & D2			
M4			Ex C3 & D3	ANCOVA		
M5	Exp B & E	Comp				
M6						

Methods

RESEARCH QUESTIONS & HYPOTHESES

	Obj I	Method	Obj II	Methods	Obj III	Methods
M1	Exp A & B	IRT2				
	$$	$$	$$	$$	$$	$$
M2	Re A & B	IRT2/3	Exp C & D	A3Z	Exp C & E	S-DENSE
	$$	$$	$$	$$	$$	$$
M3			Ex C2 & D2			
	$$	$$	$$	$$	$$	$$
M4			Ex C3 & D3	ANCOVA		
	$$	$$	$$	$$	$$	$$
M5	Exp B & E	Comp				
	$$	$$	$$			$$
M6						
	$$	$$	$$	$$	$$	$$

Budget

WORD CLOUD

Want to make sure you're sending the message you want to send? Once you have a decent draft of your proposal, copy all your text and paste it into a word cloud generator. Are the biggest words the ones you want a reader's eyes to see and hear the most often? Do they convey your message?

I did this for the first time several years ago and guess what word was the largest or the most used in my proposal?

"JUST" – the word just?!! How embarrassing! Such a weak word that tells nothing about my work. "Just fund this project" would have at least been something.

I immediately went through and eliminated almost every single "just" from my proposal. A word cloud is such a simple and wonderful way to visually catch your crutches and sharpen your sentences. Here's the word cloud for this book.

This cloud captures my message to you – work, writing, research, idea, want, can, time, start, get, good …

My advice – make a word cloud and "just" edit away!

IS IT FUNDABLE?

There are brilliant people everywhere with brilliant ideas. What makes an idea fundable?

Five fundable MUSTS.

1. Novelty

2. Grounded in the Literature (not too novel)

3. Beginning and an End

4. Measurable Impacts

5. Feasible – Supports, Facilities, People

Novelty – It's never been done before like this. That might mean with this sample, with this population, with these methods.

Grounded – Know your field deeply and how your ideas take the field a step further.

Beginning & End – So simple. Where does it start and how will you know when the program or project is finished? You won't save the world in three years but you will add value because this is now (x) and in three years it will be (x+value).

Measurable – You must be able to measure and document progress or results. Design research questions and find or develop instruments and methods to precisely answer and measure these questions.

Feasible – You are not employed by Utopia University with exceptional equipment, perfect post docs, and a non-existent teaching load. You have a great idea but need x,y,z to make it happen. Be realistic. Don't be afraid to ask for what you need to help you and the agency achieve the mission together.

DISSECT THE RFP

RFPs don't lie! Really, they don't kid around. If you were awarding a grant, of any size, would you slap something together and send it out to the world?

No, you would carefully craft your offer, describe precisely what you want, your goals, mission, budget limits, perhaps what literature influences your mission and thinking.

Think of the RFP like a job announcement. You want the job? Show them you can check almost every one of their boxes with your idea. You're answering an ad. Sell, sell, sell.

"How do you know what they *really* want?" colleagues ask. They are not trying to make it complicated, but sometimes it can feel like reading tea leaves.

How do I interpret dense RFPs?

- Review - meticulously - every line of the description. Not just the nuts and bolts stuff, like font size, page count, budget, but focus on program aims, major goals, and secondary goals.

- Any literature the agency cites in the RFP – Get it, read it, know it, use it.

- Look for language or terms used repeatedly. (e.g. Interdisciplinary, innovation, mentoring, cutting-edge, creativity, high-risk experimentation, theoretical breakthroughs, diversity.) These are clues to the agency's thinking and mission.

- Make a list of these terms. Weave these actions in your work and use these words in the proposal.

Don't gloss over the RFP terms, but don't let them consume your own ideas either. You must hold all of this in your mind at once and sculpt them simultaneously.

That said, your research questions, your ideas are the clay. Let the agency's mission help mold the method, target population, and impact. In other words, you *can* do it all and everybody wins.

"FONT CHEATER"

I am a rule follower. Or at least I'm aware of rules, which ones are important, and which can be bent from time to time.

I printed my set of proposals to review for federal agency X. I thumbed through the stack to make sure pages printed clearly. A proposal glared up at me. I knew immediately something was off. Was the font too small? The spacing too tight? Regardless, the ink coverage was denser than its competition in the stack – The font guidelines were not met.

The PI held a Full Professorship at a top research institution. Dr. Font Cheater's proposal was strong. I shared my concerns with the program officer. They printed another copy from the agency files a nd p u lled out the trusty old ruler.

Guess who got sent to the corner for cheating?

And not just sent to the corner, months of work immediately rejected for not adhering to RFP guidelines specifically font and spacing requirements.

I'm just as competitive as you and want every edge, but you MUST play within the rules stated in the RFP. Don't waste your time trying to cheat and then lose sleep worrying you'll get caught.

Just do the right thing from the beginning.

FEDERAL AGENCIES

If you're applying to a government agency the RFPs are detailed and specific. You can typically search funded projects read their abstracts and learn how much was awarded.

You can also contact a PI directly, and in my experience, they are usually kind enough to immediately send a copy of their funded proposal especially if the project is complete. In addition, you can also request copies of proposals that have been funded directly through the agency. Projects funded through tax payers' money are available to anyone requesting these through the Freedom of Information Act (FOIA).

It's also a great idea to check out funded PIs, their labs, their backgrounds. Understand your competition, research their lineup, playbook. How do you measure up?

Read all you can to understand the process in your field. Who is repeatedly getting funded? What kind of supports do they have? What are the broader impacts of their work? How are they doing this with all the time constraints?

University faculty often ask if they get can get funding even if they're only employed at a small state university and not an Ivy League school. ANYONE with a good idea can get funded. A small community non-profit, a junior college professor, and a struggling school district can all engage in that conversation with a reviewer. They all enter the arena on equal ground.

I've sat on review panels where big names with big labs and big degrees had boring ideas. The little guy can and often does win but only because they sold a big brilliant idea.

INVESTIGATE FOUNDATIONS

Private Foundations regulate themselves, have a broad range of missions and there is more variability in proposal format, requirements, budget, and feedback. Find a foundation that aligns with your mission, your work. Study mission statements. How did the foundation begin? What's their story? If this a family-run foundation, find out how funding decisions are made. What has been funded before? Do they have pet projects or locales?

Unfortunately, some Foundations have little or no communication with the PI or the institution. And even after submission the reviews are scant and so it can feel like a crap shoot.

But it's worth your time investigating upfront. Get on the phone with someone at the foundation if you can, send a paragraph about the idea you want to discuss. Develop a relationship with them. Get to know what's important to the program officer and the foundation. What does their group or family want to accomplish with the money they have been assigned to guard and distribute wisely?

Who is on their board? What are their backgrounds? Look at pictures on their webpage. What can you glean from their logo, messaging, photos, or news? How can you help them believe in you and that you will help them accomplish the foundation's work?

Unlike grants.gov and federal and state monies, private foundations control their mission and their money. Find foundations interested in your community, go meet with them, develop a relationship. Show them you care about their work and work to build their trust in you. You're on the same team.

And if they don't award your project, it's not about you, it's just not a good match currently. Never get mad at people who can give you money for work you love. Find out what changes are needed so they tag you next time.

SHOW ME THE MONEY

Everyone gets sweaty about money.

Is this too much?

Can I really ask for this?

Organizations put out RFPs because they have money they want to give you to do work that is important to them. That said, they need to fall in love with your idea and your project before they even glance at the budget.

If we rank order the cognitive load of all the tasks and pieces required for a grant submission I put budget development low on the list. In other words, play with Excel when you're tired. Number crunching is easy, writing perfect sentences - hard.

Budgets are all more similar than different. Ask another PI for a winning budget or your sponsored programs office. Use this *only* as a model. Ask your sponsored programs office for help. This is their area of expertise – money, budgets, rates. It's their job to get that stuff right prior to submission. And they will double check issues such as RFP, state, and university restrictions.

Their help gives you more time for the REAL WORK - honing those research questions, crafting the punchline, meeting with partners – and a million things SPO *cannot* do for you. Your future grant funds help support their salary. They want you to be successful. Ask for their budget expertise and ask early before you waste any of your brain time.

And please do not waste even a minute wondering if $10,000 this way or that is going to break the deal.

Round up! Obviously stay within the budget requirements. But don't think that because your budget request is $730K and the limit is $750K that you'll somehow earn brownie points.

Sell your idea first. Next be reasonable and realistic with your time and money, supplies and support to do the work proposed.

The last thing you want is to get the grant of your dreams only to beg your VP for Research to spot you $100K to complete the project as promised.

BUDGET JUSTIFICATION

The budget justification is low on the cognitive load list as is the budget creation. Do this when you're tired too. Your proposal will make the budgeted needs (e.g. lab supplies, equipment, assistantships) clear but this is where you have space to expand a bit.

Add a little more explanation why you need model X over model Y even though it's twice the price. Describe your teaching load if necessary and what percentage of buyout time is needed to do the work. This should of course correspond with your proposal's timeline chart and data collection timeline.

And remember at this point the reviewers already have significant interest in your work, so be bold about why you need this or that. What will that post doc do and learn under your direction? How will your program impact future researchers and research in your field? How will the pricey consultant from University Z inform and benefit your research?

If you work at a state institution, an underfunded non-profit there is not shame in asking for paper or copy costs on a large proposal. Request what is needed to do the work, otherwise all those little things will have to come from somewhere and it might be your own pocket in a pinch – I speak from experience here.

PART THREE

ATTITUDE

A general way of thinking and feeling about something.

DESIGN LIKE AN ENTREPRENEUR

What does an entrepreneur do? They start small with limited funds. They take calculated risks. They go-off the trail sometimes. They try new ideas, test them out, and build diverse teams to generate new ideas and prototypes.

Academic freedom and a university position provide some security for risk taking and edgy entrepreneurship. And university start-up funds help support building a laboratory, developing a research group, traveling to conferences, collaborating, and building a systemic path for work and exploration.

I had little financial support, so I had to make a lot from little. Designing like an entrepreneur can help get your work off the ground through pilot work, small data sets, meetings for potential partners. And use your own time as efficiently as possible.

Think of yourself as a research entrepreneur as you grow your business.

Your business is earning grant monies so you can do the work you love.

START-UP MENTALITY

Agencies are typically not going to fund simply the next stepping stone in your line of research. They want to be part of something ground-breaking, innovative, and work that is the "start of something." The next step in your research might be all of these things, but you need to frame it as such. It needs to be sold as the start of something new.

Along with being the "start of something," the Start-Up mentality goes to the notion of doing pilot work to have some initial data to present in the proposal. Test the waters as a budding business venture would do. Do it lean and efficiently so that if it fails, you make adjustments and have some time and funds for a redo. Everyone should leave room for a do over! Mistakes happen at the beginning and better to get them out of the way before the big funding comes. And even better, then the agency knows you have thought out your plan, your methods, and have a handful of examples where it worked already on the books.

GRANT WRITING EGO

I've read many a proposal that almost sound apologetic. They were not fun to read and could not have been fun to craft.

Grow your grant writing ego now.

You're an entrepreneur, a researcher.

You're a dreamer, a designer, a doer.

You are poised to help a big agency find and fund great work you both believe in. Together you will develop a magnificent thing!

BUY TIME

People say to me all the time …

"Grant writing is so hard."

"It takes so much time."

"I'll probably get rejected again."

But what if you don't? What if you up your game this time? Don't cut and paste from some old proposal – by the way that has never worked for me. Old text might help get you started – it gets some letters on the screen – but it's old, period.

But if you do write a winning grant, you *buy your time*.

Time to do the work you want to do.

Time to read.

Time to think.

Time to write.

Time is my commodity. With grant money you set your own schedule. You are committed to meeting the promises of your proposal, but you set the schedule. If you like a morning swim at 10am to stay healthy and focused so be it. If late nights in the lab make you groove, it's on.

Grant money provides flexibility and the support to do the work you think is great. Time must be invested up front, long hours, deep thinking, hard edits. But a five-year funded research program is the prize. Summer support, post docs, travel, collaboration, publications, and conferences to feed the academic mind. Go eat!

FINDING FLOW

Do you ever lose track of time while deep in your work? Forget the hour when you're in the lab? Lose time crunching data? Writing code?

This is *flow*. Get there with your writing as much as you can.

I have entire grant proposals I don't fully remember crafting.

Get so deep in the work you think of nothing else. And find other activities that help you focus and get you deep into flow. Flow will become a more usual and natural state.

What are the conditions and factors that help you get there?

- Exercise
- Coffee
- Pleasure reading
- Reading in field
- Walk in fresh air

You are the test subject. You are the specimen. Set the conditions, flow, repeat. Set the habit, fight the resistance to work. The resistance to writing is real, and it's fierce. Words on the paper can seem so intimidating and final.

But writing is always a work-in-progress as are we, the writers.

So, study yourself. What works best for you? What inputs get you to produce the outputs you desire? Put in the time to develop your habit, the routine. Crack the nut and create flow-inducing environments for your body and your mind.

HABITS START SLOW

If you are a tenure track faculty member – there are so many distractions pulling you from the real work. The resistance to writing papers, writing grant proposals is fierce ... Grade papers, attend meetings, hold office hours, lunch with colleagues about new policies, call with your mentor, journal articles to read from last month, faculty senate, exercise, feed kids, feed self, more meetings ... fierce I tell you.

Bad habits die slow, good ones start slow.

I'm writing this on the sidelines during my daughter's soccer practice. But understanding your own habits and constraints will help you find productive windows of writing time.

One semester I found myself quite grumpy on Wednesdays. All day – a funk. When planning my teaching schedule, the following Spring I realized it was the class I was teaching Wednesday evening. I was allowing that one class to suck my energy and affect productivity all day.

Make a list of your work and writing habits each day of the week. Include commute, office hours, email, lunches, carpool wait time, classes, exercise, hobbies, ...

Where does all that time go?

Look at your list, which days and times are your most productive? Why? Which are not and to what can you attribute the lull? Are there certain places where you are more in your flow? Are there mentors or colleagues who boost your creativity? Think about the last six months what was your most productive period and why? When can you make 10 minutes in each day to write and sketch new ideas?

WORK-LIFE: GRAB TIME!

Don't wait until you have a whole day "to write." Grab time when you can. Sketch ideas, draft research questions, call a colleague to brainstorm, and write, write, write.

Every moment holds a new idea, new insight, new connections.

Sometimes ideas seem to come out of nowhere. And they often come when you're "not at work."

Over wine after our Wednesday evening classes, a psychology professor and I chatted about our research and specifically measurement tools. I joked about how similar my toddler was to the chimps she was studying – learning to share is difficult for us all. A terrific research collaboration began that has now led to several publications and over a million dollars in research monies. It's all thanks to a good Pinot Noir and reaching across the silos and diving deep into the intricacies of our work.

Too often conversations with our colleagues devolve into university politics or student issues or personal banter. We often miss the opportunity for meaningful conversations with the minds around us.

"Great mind discuss ideas.
Average minds discuss events.
Small minds discuss people."

~ Eleanor Roosevelt

Be open and vulnerable enough to discuss what you're really struggling to understand. Every researcher is struggling to understand something. If they're not, they're not a scientist.

Similarly, conversations with other parents or the cashier at the grocery store can spark my thinking about ways to improve student recruitment, manage new grad students, and even data flow.

Don't shut off the scientific mind and idea flow outside the office.

WRITING IS KING

My father-in-law, a government scientist had over 300 publications.

"How do you keep it up Jerry?"

"If I don't write about my experiments nobody knows what I've done."

So simple.

Writing is king.

If you don't communicate and ask for money nobody knows you need it. If you don't leave a record or body of research nobody knows you did it.

Be a researcher who writes.

Regardless of field – Write papers, write protocols, write grant proposals. Don't just make lists, flesh out outlines, make great sentences.

Working and practicing your writing is never wasted time.

Want to write lean athletic prose?

Practice.

Write what you know.

What did you have for dinner last night? Write 3-4 sentences right here. Make them good. Make me jealous and want to order that exact same pizza, try that curry dish or use Cuban oregano tonight. When you're done, read it aloud ... with a dash of snooty voice if desired. Did it make you salivate?

COGNITIVE LOAD

Writing is taxing. The cognitive load high. Track your energy and decide when you have the most – early morning, late nights, after exercise – Write during these times of focus.

An RFP might require a variety of components ranging from budget justification to letters of support to project abstract. They do not all haul the same cognitive load. Over the years I've learned to do low cognitive tasks when I'm distracted, waiting in a carpool line, or hit the wall in the project description.

Below is a rough list of how I think about the grant writing components with respect to load and difficulty. This of course varies for different projects, and different people, but it's a general guide that works for me.

Always keep a few "easy" things on the to-do list so you can feel productive about some bit right now.

PROPOSAL COMPONENTS RANKED HIGH TO LOW

	Challenge	Pay Off
Abstract	Succinct	A small taste
Project Summary	What belongs?	A good bite
Introduction	Punchline	Hook 'em
Research Questions	Every word matters	Heart of the work
Literature Review	Density	Roadmap
Method	Specificity	Plans well laid
Analysis	Predicting Data	Illustrate Hypotheses
Mentoring Plan	Make Meaningful	Important Work
Letters of Support	Use different voices	Building partnerships
Data Management	Predict and protect data	Organization
Charts & Figures	Eye appeal, visual summary	Fun and look good!
Budget	Attention to detail	The spending!
Budget Justification	Explaining the need	The spending!

START TIMES

A body at rest will remain at rest unless an outside force acts on it ... like a deadline!

Or better yet, set a start time. When I set a start time, I can live in the moment, my moment doing whatever I want to do – eating popsicles, reading a journal article, writing a research plan.

I set a start time – "Tomorrow at 7:30am I'll start on that new budget." Then I can let myself enjoy the evening with my family instead of semi-thinking about graduate student stipends while trying to listen to a story about who pushed who in the lunch line today.

I am more present and able to experience and feel the peace and depth of now. This is life too – right now! You are choosing to read this book

Writing a grant proposal is not typically a weekend chore like opening the pool this season. Instead it is a long-term conversation writers have with themselves. We struggle to shape and develop scenes, characters, and structure. All of this simmers ... or festers.

I've done most of my grant writing with two children in my midst. I carve brief 10-30 minute periods while at my daughter's piano lesson, waiting for the coffee to brew, or while the soccer team warms up. These quick windows can be exceedingly productive. I also use larger chunks of time but I set start times. I've seen colleagues in academia fail because they teach, grade, prepare their classes, but "Friday is my writing day." FRIDAY is too much time and pressure. It's overwhelming to write all day, any day. Instead of sprinting all day Friday, jog around the block regularly.

Setting start times for any work – "10am I'll work on that method section" - allows us to do other tasks, whatever they may be – making dinner, reading, playing with the kids, grading – and focus on living, feeling, and breathing.

If we live well, we write well.

Being present brings clarity and meaning to our moments and also later when crafting ideas into fundable programs of research.

STOP TIMES

Equally important as scheduling start times is planning to stop. It might sound counter intuitive, but after a chunk of time of writing, sketching, or reading I stop when I have a great idea or list of ideas. It might be a new line of literature to include, partnership idea, or clarity about an experiment schedule. I go for a walk, swim, play piano … anything to stretch another part of my brain. Then I'm eager to get back to the document next time. It gives me a place to get started.

When stop times are planned, it's easier to get started.

What often happens is writers are sprinting so hard getting it all out at once and end the writing period exhausted and uninterested in returning. Instead create little carrots that draw you back. "Oooh I want to bring in some of Wynn's work right here and that section needs some reorganizing too." Now I have my to-do list for my next writing window. I know where to go in the document and won't waste 20 minutes floundering.

Stop early so you can start ready.

Just like weight training, lifting the maximum for three days will haunt your muscles, making day four a struggle, and the following day requires rest. Grant development is a marathon not a sprint.

BE REALISTIC

Friends ask me to read their grant proposals.

"Do you think I'm doing enough?"

"Is this enough for that much money?"

Nobody's going to save the world with a $10 million grant. You're certainly not going to do it with $500K. Do not over promise or beg. Agencies and reviewers have a strong handle on what is realistic and as a proposer you must do the same. What can you fully accomplish in the funding period? Are you accounting for the time required for data analyses and peer reviewed publications? A realistic plan of activities – incubation, hiring graduate assistants, data collection, analyses, and writing – should be sketched, charted, and plotted to keep you grounded – Be realistic and stay realistic. Otherwise regret and horrific stress will cloud your award, "Oh no! I got the money and have to do ALL that work. That's impossible!"

BE RISKY

I enjoy reading and reviewing proposals out of field. It stretches my mind and teaches me about cutting edge research I would otherwise never encounter.

If you share your proposal with a distant peer in a different field, they should be absolutely wowed by your plan because the whole proposal is scientific news. These are not methods or species he's familiar with, so it should be interesting and even exciting to a peer scientist.

If you're not wowing your peer in the next building, you certainly won't wow someone in your field.

New PIs are often afraid of being too risky.

There should be a good balance of risk in your proposed experiments. Maybe one of the three experiments will produce predictable solid results that build upon your previous published work or dissertation, but the other two are higher risk, higher potential, greater overall impact. *These academic risks are where a reviewer will get truly intrigued and invested in your work* because it's a new idea that contributes to as well as stretches the field.

Depending on the agency you're applying to, significant levels of risk are tolerated and even encouraged. No one wants to fund the next predictable thing? So, propose to put a few bricks in the wall but then point way up and make the reader see the magnificent potential.

CRITICAL CRITICS

Writing is extremely personal. Right now, I'm thinking about what you think of the words I'm typing. I'm worried you might think I'm an idiot. And when I hit send and share a work in progress with a colleague or a mentor I'm still usually wincing when I do so.

Sharing our writing makes us feel vulnerable. Even when it's science writing. Words are personal and powerful.

Imposter syndrome sneaks up all the time. You need to remind yourself this is hard work intellectually and emotionally. But only *you* can express your big idea. And in the act and practice of writing - your research questions and your methods section and literature mapping will all grow stronger and clearer.

The act of writing will build your confidence and your research programs.

No matter how hard it is to share your writing, you must. Another set of eyes – critical eyes to give real feedback on content, structure, analyses – are all invaluable.

Assemble a small writing group to exchange proposals or target a handful of people to help you with different facets of the proposal. Ask them to tear it apart. This is not personal, it's business.

"UNFORTUNATELY"

Friday night 8:55. There m ust b e a q ueue o f e mails from the National Science Foundation headed out to unsuspecting PIs. A dinner with my family, a glass of wine, about to relax with a good book, and there it is - The "unfortunately" email.

I don't read past that word.

I know what it's referring to. I've been waiting for months for the news on a new proposal.

Call it self-preservation, deflection, defiance. I am never in the mood to read reviews at that time. It might even take a week before I am ready to scroll through the feedback.

I let collaborators know the bad news immediately, but do not wallow.

One group of reviewers didn't buy your idea. That doesn't mean your idea is not worthy. However, you need to make some changes. When you're ready – *really ready* and well caffeinated – print them out and read through every word of each review.

Remember reviews are not personal, it's business. You need to do a better job of selling your idea and your team's capacity to get the work done or move on to your next idea.

DON'T linger in "unfortunately" land.

DON'T blame the "stupid reviewers who just didn't get it!"

DON'T be angry.

Every successful grant writer has a pile of "Unfortunately" letters. Welcome to the club!

POST REVIEW

DO dissect reviewers' comments.

DO use worthy criticism going forward.

DO chuck reviews that seem mean spirited – that business is about them, not you.

DO make changes before resubmitting, but only those changes *you* believe strengthen the work.

DON'T be angry - that gains nothing.

DON'T give up - that gains nothing.

DON'T doubt yourself - that gains nothing.

REVIEWS

A question I always get asked in workshops, "How do you deal with negative reviews?"

I'm of course completely academic and logical about the whole peer review process, using every morsel of wisdom the reviewers have so graciously shared with me. I'm enlightened and a better person for their critiques. (You read that with the intended sarcasm, I hope.)

In truth … I probably go through something resembling the stages of grief.

- **Shock**
  They didn't love my idea? How is that possible?Did they use the right email? Who could they have funded if not me?

- **Denial**
  I already shared with you my "Unfortunately" email reaction. This is probably more deflection and parsing the news into bites my brain can consume productively. I use the "Unfortunately" email as information. That project was not funded - now I can use brain space thinking about something else. I'll get to the reviews when needed and my curiosity outweighs disappointment.

- **Anger**

  This can happen when I read the reviews, but it's more of an eye rolling anger, not a "throw-computer-out-office-window" anger. And those eye-rolls are sometimes aimed at myself, knowing they are spot on, or that I had thought of that but simply didn't make time. Besides, this is a game. I can't win every match. I also know most reviewers are just like me and they are truly trying to help guide the PI in the resubmission process.

  But every once and a while you get some loon who has to get on the high horse and be an ass. They're probably just having a bad day or are teaching "that class" tonight, I tell myself. It's not about me or my brilliant idea. One of my mottos taken from the wonderful book "The Four Agreements" by Don Miguel Ruiz is to never take anything personally. Use the helpful feedback and quality criticism. The rest - simply discard.

- **Bargaining**

  This is the phase where I might start to tell myself perhaps the RFP was not a perfect fit for this work. Maybe the agency or foundation has slightly shifted in their mission and is no longer a good outlet. Maybe I'm not deeply in love with the project or my team members anymore. I feel some relief.

- **Reconstruction**

  Then there's a spark somewhere. A comment from one of the reviewers I savor. A literature connection kindly suggested. A new intersection I hadn't seen before. And I start building again. It might be with notes I highlighted from the reviewers. It might be some encouragement provided by the program officer in a cover letter. Or it might be starting a new project entirely.

- **Hope**

  I start thinking about entering the arena again. I look at what was funded. I'm inspired by the great work that's being supported, a little envious to not be in the winners' circle, but know my ideas are still in the ballpark.

  And as I like to say after a loss, I'm due for a win now! Dig in!

Now you're ready - Get writing!

Visit my page JulieCwikla.com where I've posted some grant development resources. Some of these I use in my Good to Great Grant Writing workshops or with writing teams. And others are just quick ways and shortcuts to strengthen your grant writing game.

Enter this code: "GoodToGreat" for free access.

And know I'll be updating the files regularly as I keep upping my game too. So check back and please drop a note to let me know what you think of my Secrets to Success Julie.Cwikla@gmail.com. I'm also active on LinkedIn and Twitter @JulieCwikla - come say hello.

If you found this book helpful please give a minute to leave a quick review on Amazon and share with your colleagues.

*Keep the prose lean and strong, and
good luck in your next competition!*

Made in the USA
Middletown, DE
01 September 2023

37774983R00046